The Scientists Behind

Earth's Processes

Andrew Solway

www.raintreepublishers.co.uk
Visit our website to find out more information about Raintree books.

To order:
☎ Phone 0845 6044371
🖨 Fax +44 (0) 1865 312263
💻 Email myorders@raintreepublishers.co.uk

Customers from outside the UK please telephone +44 1865 312262

Raintree is an imprint of Capstone Global Library Limited, a company incorporated in England and Wales having its registered office at 7 Pilgrim Street, London, EC4V 6LB – Registered company number: 6695582

Edited by Andrew Farrow, Adam Miller, and Diyan Leake
Designed by Philippa Jenkins
Original illustrations © Capstone Global Library Limited 2011
Illustrated by sprout.uk.com Limited and Capstone Global Library Limited
Picture research by Hannah Taylor
Originated by Capstone Global Library Limited
Printed and bound in China by CTPS

ISBN 978 1 406 22057 5 (hardback)
14 13 12 11 10
10 9 8 7 6 5 4 3 2 1

British Library Cataloguing in Publication Data
Solway, Andrew.
 The scientists behind Earth's processes. -- (Sci-hi)
 551'.0922-dc22
A full catalogue record for this book is available from the British Library.

Acknowledgements
The author and publishers are grateful to the following for permission to reproduce copyright material: Alamy Images pp. **13** bottom (© David Robertson), **14** (© Arctic Images), **17** (© The Natural History Museum); Claudia Alexander p. **41**; Corbis pp. **4** (Louie Psihoyos), **11** (Hulton-Deutsch Collection), **12** (Image Source), **13** top (Bettmann), **25** top (Jonathan Blair), **38** (Jim Sugar); D. Curling/Physics Department/University of Toronto p. **32**; Getty Images p. **31** bottom (National Geographic/Emory Kristof), istockphoto p. **21** (© landbysea); NASA pp. **5**, **40**; NOAA p. **28**; Reuters p. **18** (Barry Huang); Science Photo Library pp. **19** (Christian Darkin), **22**, **26** (Christian Darkin), **31** top (P. Rona/Oar/National Undersea Research program/NOAA); Science Photo Library pp. **34** (NASA), **35** (Worldsat International), **36** (Emilio Segre Visual Archives/American Institute of Physics), **37** (Scott Camazine), **39** (Lawrence Berkeley National Laboratory/Gary Strand, NCAR); shutterstock background images and design elements throughout, **contents page** top (© Tonis Pan), **contents page** bottom (© Kushch Dmitry), pp. **6–7** (© Kushch Dmitry), **15** (© Tonis Pan); Copyright Marie Tharp 1977/2003. Reproduced with permission of Marie Tharp Maps LLC, 8 Edward Street, Sparkill, New York 10976 p. **30**; TopFoto pp. **9** (The Granger Collection), **25** bottom (Imagno/Austrian Archives), **29** (The Granger Collection).

Main cover photograph of Xu Xing, Chinese dinosaur fossil hunter, reproduced with permission of Corbis (Xinhua Photo); inset cover photograph of a snowman reproduced with permission of shutterstock (© Margaret M. Stewart).

The publisher would like to thank literary consultant Marla Conn and content consultant Suzy Gazlay for their assistance in the preparation of this book.

Disclaimer

Contents

Introduction   4

The beginnings of geology   6

Glaciers and climate change   12

Life in the rocks   16

Journey to the centre of the Earth   20

Lands on the move   24

Mountains in the ocean   28

Plate tectonics   32

Predicting the weather   36

What next?   40

Timeline   42

Quick quiz   44

Glossary   45

Find out more   46

Index   48

What is Snowball Earth? Find out on page 15!

How old is Earth? Turn to page 6 to find out!

Some words are shown in bold, **like this**. These words are explained in the glossary. You will find important information and definitions underlined, <u>like this</u>.

INTRODUCTION

Earth has existed for over 4 billion years. Over that time it has seen huge changes in **climate**, in the air, and in the shape of the land. Humans have been on Earth for only 2 million years or so. It is only in the last 200–300 years that we have begun to understand the processes that shape Earth.

STUDYING ROCKS

Much of what we know about the early Earth has come from studying rocks. Rock scientists are known as **geologists**.

Geologists have learned how landscapes form and change. They have found the causes of earthquakes and volcanoes and they know how to measure the ages of rocks. Geologists have also discovered that the continents are not as solid and fixed as we once thought.

Rocks hold clues to life on Earth in the past. This scientist is unearthing a dinosaur fossil.

Satellite images are one of many tools used by meteorologists to predict the movement of hurricanes and other weather.

PHOTOGRAPHING THE WEATHER

This is Hurricane Ivan, photographed from space in 2004. Satellites circling Earth are vital for modern research into the weather and climate. Studying pictures like this is part of the science that helps us understand more about Earth's processes.

OTHER EARTH SCIENTISTS

Other scientists study Earth in different ways. **Palaeontologists** study **fossils** to learn about the history of life on Earth. **Meteorologists** study the weather. They have developed ways to **forecast** events such as hurricanes and storms. **Climatologists** study the climate (the average weather over many years). They have learned a lot about past climates and can make predictions about the climate in the future.

Read on!

In this book you can learn about the lives and work of scientists who have helped uncover Earth's secrets.

- Which scientist thinks that Earth might once have been a "snowball"?
- Who found the biggest mountain range in the world – under water?
- Who found evidence that there might be life on other planets?

Read on to find out!

THE BEGINNINGS OF GEOLOGY

In the late 1700s, many scientists linked ideas about Earth and rock formation with the history of the world described in the Bible. They accepted the belief that Earth had been formed about 6,000 years ago. Many scientists at that time thought that Earth's rocks were formed during the time of Noah's Flood, a worldwide flood described in the Bible.

AN OLDER EARTH

In the 1920s, the English geologist Arthur Holmes developed a way to work out how old rocks really are. He measured the tiny amounts of **radioactive** material found in some rocks. He used his measurements to work out that Earth was 4 billion years old.

In 1953 the US scientist Clair Cameron Patterson (1922–1995) used rocks from a meteorite to get a more accurate age for Earth. He dated it as 4.55 billion years old. This estimate is generally accepted today.

In the Grand Canyon, the Colorado River has cut deep into the Earth, exposing layers of rock going back millions of years.

ROCKS FROM WATER

The German scientist Abraham Werner suggested that the whole Earth was originally water, with small particles floating in it. The particles settled as **sediments** (layers), with the bigger particles settling first. Over time, each layer was compressed (squashed) by the sediments above it. The layers gradually turned into rocks that rose out of the water.

Werner thought that the oldest rock layers formed at the beginning of the world. People believed this was around 4000 BC. Newer layers formed during the time of Noah's Flood. Since then, hardly any new rocks had formed.

Some of Werner's ideas were very sensible. Some rocks do form from sediments as he suggested – they are called **sedimentary rocks**. The problem was that Werner did not back up his ideas with evidence. He did not look closely at rock formations to see what they were really like.

DISAGREEING WITH WERNER

James Hutton, a Scottish scientist, did look at rocks carefully. He observed that in many places, rocks were not arranged in neat layers. Some rocks seemed to push up into the layers of rock above them. In one place, Hutton found layers of grey rock that had thin "veins" of a very different, red rock running through them. He argued that the red rock must have flowed into the grey rocks as a liquid, filling cracks and gaps, and then turning solid.

Everywhere he looked, Hutton found evidence that some rocks were liquid when they formed. He suggested that these rocks are formed by heat from deep inside the Earth. Today we call this kind of rock igneous rock.

SEASHELLS ON HILLS

Hutton also suggested an answer to another problem. Some sedimentary rocks containing fossils of sea animals are found high on the tops of hills. How did they get there? Hutton did not know for certain, but he thought that heat from below ground could play a part. Perhaps heat from deep under ground could push up whole areas of sedimentary rock. This is what modern geologists call **uplift**.

JAMES HUTTON

LIVED: 1726–1797

NATIONALITY: Scottish

FAMOUS FOR: Showing that rocks could be formed by heat, and for his "Theory of the Earth" (see page 10) that brought together the basic processes of geology.

DID YOU KNOW? Hutton was a member of the Philosophical Society of Edinburgh. He was usually lively and entertaining company. But when he had to give a talk to the Society on his Theory of the Earth, he was so nervous he got sick. His friend Joseph Black had to do the talk for him.

Find out more about Hutton's Theory of the Earth on the next page ...

THEORY OF THE EARTH

In 1785 Hutton put together all his observations and ideas into something he called the Theory of the Earth. He rejected the idea that most rocks were formed during Noah's Flood. He believed that rocks are continually being formed, broken down, and made again. This whole process is known today as the rock cycle.

Hutton also had new ideas about the age of Earth. He thought it must have taken millions of years, not thousands, for rocks to wear down and re-form into the landscapes we see today.

THE ROCK CYCLE

Rocks on Earth's surface are continually worn away by rain, snow, wind, and ice. This process is called weathering. The tiny pieces of weathered rock are carried away by the wind or in rivers. This process is called erosion.

Many of these rock pieces reach the ocean, where they begin to form new rocks. The rocks may then be pushed to the surface by uplift. At the surface, the rocks are once again affected by weathering and erosion. The cycle then continues.

SPREADING HUTTON'S IDEAS

Hutton's ideas were not widely accepted during his lifetime. However, in the 1830s and 40s another geologist made them famous. Charles Lyell travelled the world studying rocks. In 1830 he published a book called *Principles of Geology*. He used Hutton's theories to describe different kinds of rocks and explain how they formed. The book became a bestseller, and made Lyell famous.

CHARLES LYELL

LIVED: 1797–1875

NATIONALITY: Scottish

FAMOUS FOR: Writing the book *Principles of Geology* and promoting geology around the world

DID YOU KNOW? In his time, Lyell was a "rock" superstar. In 1841 he was paid $2,000 (about $40,000 in modern terms) to do a lecture tour of the United States. Thousands of people paid high prices for tickets for his lectures.

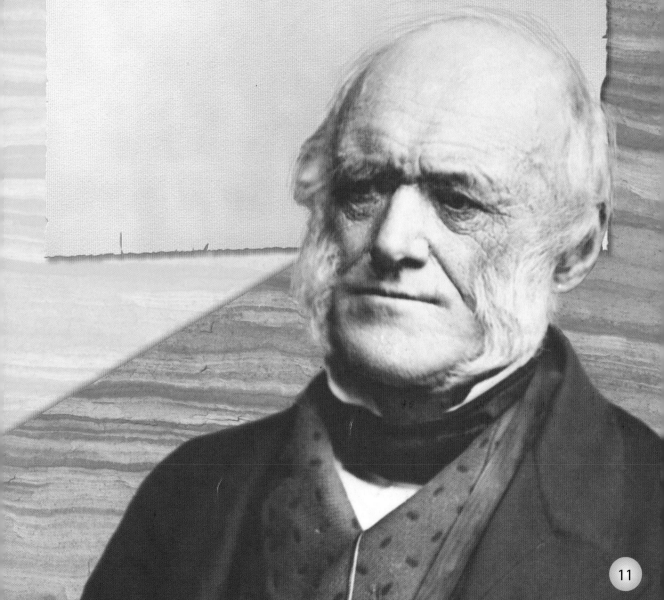

GLACIERS
and climate change

Around the time that Charles Lyell was writing about Hutton's ideas, a professor called Louis Agassiz was studying glaciers in the Swiss mountains. His studies led to the discovery that Earth's climate was very different in the past.

Louis Agassiz was a naturalist who studied the living world, rather than an earth scientist. He studied fish and other animals. However, in 1836 he decided to spend some time studying glaciers. He built a hut on the ice, and spent four years studying the Aar glacier and its surroundings. He also collected information on glaciers from other scientists and mountaineers.

As glaciers flow slowly downhill, they grind the mountains away, leaving their imprint on the rocks.

LOUIS AGASSIZ

LIVED: 1807–1873

NATIONALITY: Born Swiss, later American

FAMOUS FOR: Finding evidence from glaciers and rocks that there was an ice age on Earth thousands of years ago

DID YOU KNOW? As well as studying glaciers, Agassiz was one of the great biologists of his time. However, he never accepted Darwin's theory of evolution. He believed that animal and plant species were fixed, and could not change over time.

GLACIERS WERE HERE

Agassiz noted that many valleys in the Swiss mountains are U-shaped, with a flat bottom and steep sides. This valley shape is produced when a glacier flows through a valley. However, most of the U-shaped valleys did not have glaciers in them. He found that many rocks were covered in scratches, just like the scratches caused by glaciers as they flow slowly down a valley.

Agassiz also learned about huge boulders called erratics, which were very different from the rocks around them. He suggested that these rocks had been carried down the valley by a glacier and then dumped when it melted.

A PAST ICE AGE

Agassiz concluded that a few thousand years in the past, the whole of Switzerland must have been covered by a huge ice cap, similar to the ice cap over Greenland today. He suggested that Earth must have gone through a "Great Ice Age", when it was much colder everywhere.

This erratic boulder in Scotland is evidence that there were glaciers here in the past.

13

PAST CLIMATES

Agassiz found evidence that there had been an ice age thousands of years ago. Modern scientists can plot changes in Earth's climate going back millions of years. The evidence comes from many different sources. The growth rings of trees give us information about the climate over the last few thousand years.

Ice from the Antarctic can also tell us about climate changes. <u>Scientists drill down and take out long cylinders of ice called ice cores. They can look at layers in the ice cores going back almost a million years</u>. As ice forms, bubbles of air are trapped in it. Scientists can look at the oxygen in these bubbles to learn about the climate at the time.

Going even further back, scientists can find evidence about the ancient climate from rocks. The chemicals in different rock layers, and the fossils found in the rocks, give us a lot of information about whether the climate in the past was hot or cold, dry or wet.

Tiny bubbles in ice cores provide information about the climate going back thousands of years.

NOT JUST ONE ICE AGE

All this research has shown that there was not just one great ice age. There have been many ice ages in the past. These stretch back over a billion years. We are currently in an ice age that began about 2½ million years ago. Within this ice age there have been colder periods (glacials) and warmer periods (interglacials). The "Ice Age" that Agassiz discovered was the most recent glacial period, which happened 15,000–20,000 years ago.

THE OLDEST ICE CORE

In 2004 a team of scientists from ten countries finished an eight-year project in the Antarctic. They drilled down more than 3 kilometres (nearly 2 miles) to get an ice core. The ice core shows that in the last 800,000 years there have been eight glacials. During these times, ice sheets spread across northern Europe and North America.

In 1989 US geologist Joe Kirschvink suggested that between 850 and 630 million years ago there was a very cold "super" ice age. During this period the whole of Earth was covered by a vast ice sheet. He called this the "Snowball Earth" theory.

LIFE IN THE ROCKS

Louis Agassiz did some of his most important studies on fish fossils. Fossils are the remains of living things captured in rocks. Earth scientists use fossils to trace the history of life back millions of years. They can also use fossils to help date rocks.

FOSSILS FOR DATING

The idea of working out the date of rocks from their fossils came from an Englishman named William Smith. Smith was a surveyor: he helped build canals and mines. This gave him plenty of opportunity to look at rocks. He noticed that he could find similar rocks in different parts of the country. He wondered whether there was a way he could be sure that similar-looking rocks were actually from the same period in the past.

Smith showed that many sedimentary rocks have a fossil "signature". Certain kinds of fossil are found in rocks from that period, wherever they are in the world. He was able to use fossil signatures to sort sedimentary rocks into date order.

<u>If rocks are undisturbed, the older strata (layers) are found below the more recent ones</u>. Sometimes whole sections of rock get tilted, squashed, or turned over completely. Smith's technique of fossil signatures makes it possible to tell older rocks from younger ones, even when the strata have become tilted or bent.

This is a picture from William Smith's book listing the kinds of fossil found in different types of rock.

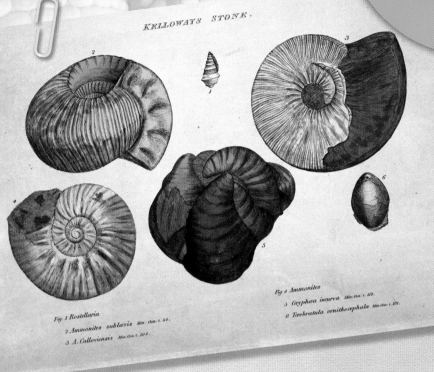

KELLOWAYS STONE.

Fig. 1 Rostellaria
2 Ammonites sublævis Min. Con. t. 54.
3 A. Callovienzis Min. Con. t. 104.

Fig 4 Ammonites
5 Gryphæa incurva Min. Con. t. 112.
6 Terebratula ornithocephala Min. Con. t. 101.

WILLIAM SMITH

LIVED: 1769–1839

NATIONALITY: British

FAMOUS FOR: Showing how fossils could be used to date rocks. He also produced the first geological map of Britain, showing the different types of surface rock.

DID YOU KNOW? At school, Smith and his school friends played marbles with small round stones called "pundlibs". These "stones" were actually fossils of shellfish.

Turn the page to find out more about fossils ...

RECORDS OF ANCIENT LIFE

Smith was interested in fossils as a way to date rocks. He was not so interested in the fossils themselves. <u>Large numbers of fossils first appear in rocks about 545 million years old</u>. The fossils suggest that complex, multicellular animals (made from many cells) appeared at this time.

The fossil animals that are studied the most first appeared about 230 million years ago and disappeared about 65 million years ago. These were the dinosaurs. Dinosaur fossils were first found in the 1820s. Scientists then believed that dinosaurs were slow, heavy, reptile-like creatures. However, as scientists have learned more, this view has changed. Some dinosaurs were fast-moving, warm-blooded animals. They are thought to be the ancestors of birds.

This photo shows the palaeontologist Xu Xing examining a bird-like fossil discovered in 2010.

HOW DINOSAURS BECAME BIRDS

The connection between dinosaurs and birds has only become clear in the last 20 years. Xu Xing is a Chinese palaeontologist, studying living things from the past. He has done more than most scientists to make that connection. Since 1997 he has discovered more than 30 new dinosaurs. Many of these dinosaurs had feathers, and some had wings. The oldest bird-like dinosaur was *Anchiornis*. It lived about 160 million years ago. Another dinosaur, *Microraptor*, was only about 60 centimetres (2 feet) long and had four wings.

This image shows what Microraptor may have looked like. Even with its extra wings, it could only glide.

PUTTING COLOURS TO DINOSAURS

Early in 2010, a group of scientists, including Xu Xing, worked out the actual colours of some dinosaur feathers. The team looked at fossil feathers under the microscope and compared them with modern bird feathers of different colours. Using this technique, they were able to work out what colours the fossil feathers were. Another group of researchers worked out the complete colour scheme for *Anchiornis*, the fossil that Xu Xing discovered in 2009.

JOURNEY TO THE
CENTRE OF THE EARTH

In the 1700s, James Hutton showed that deep under ground it must be hot enough to melt rocks. Volcanoes are clear evidence for this. Two hundred years later, scientists still understood little about the Earth deep beneath their feet.

LEARNING FROM EARTHQUAKES

When earthquakes happen, the shaking produces **seismic waves** (shock waves) in the rocks. The waves travel down into the ground. Some waves go right through the Earth. Others travel less distance and do not go down so deep.

In the early 1900s, earth scientists realized they could learn about the structure of Earth from seismic waves. In 1909 Andrija Mohorovičić (An-dree-ya Mo-horo-vich-ich) showed that there was a sudden change as waves passed from the **crust** of Earth into deeper rocks (the **mantle**). In 1913 Beno Gutenberg used seismic waves to measure the size of the **core** at the centre of Earth.

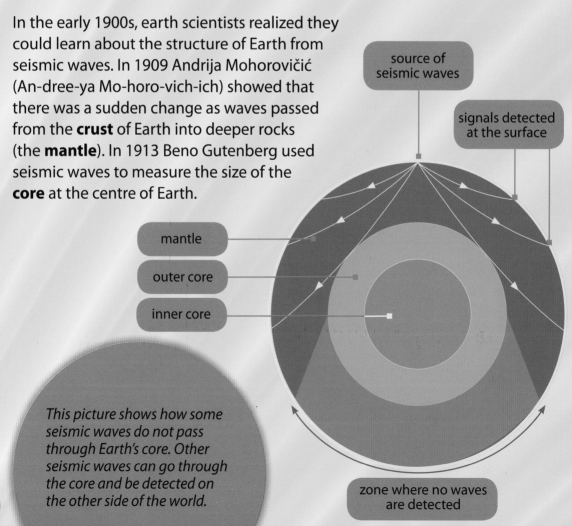

source of seismic waves

signals detected at the surface

mantle

outer core

inner core

This picture shows how some seismic waves do not pass through Earth's core. Other seismic waves can go through the core and be detected on the other side of the world.

zone where no waves are detected

DRILLING DEEP

Seismic waves tell us a lot, but scientists have also tried to get direct evidence of Earth's structure by drilling through the crust. The deepest hole drilled so far is the Kola Superdeep Borehole. It was drilled by a team of Russian scientists. Between 1963 and 1994 the team drilled down over 12 kilometres (7½ miles). At this depth the rocks became so hot that it was impossible to keep the drill cool.

On the seabed, Earth's crust is much thinner than on land – about 6 kilometres (4 miles) thick. Scientific drilling ships like this one are trying to bore down through the crust to reach the mantle.

GENIUS OF SEISMIC WAVES

Inge Lehmann was a Danish seismologist who was the world expert at understanding seismic waves. From 1928 until 1953 she was in charge of all earthquake recordings in Denmark. Lehmann called herself "the only seismologist in Denmark" as a joke, because Denmark has so few earthquakes. In fact, for many years she did work alone, without anyone to help her even with office work.

Although there were only a few small earthquakes in Denmark, Lehmann's seismographs (detectors for picking up seismic waves) were often busy. They picked up seismic waves from earthquakes as far away as New Zealand. Lehmann became expert at working out what the seismograph readings meant.

During one strong earthquake in New Zealand, Lehmann noticed that seismic waves were appearing in places where they were not expected. She looked at the waves recorded in other places around Europe and found similar results. Lehmann thought that the unusual waves were bouncing off a boundary within Earth's core. She showed that Earth's core is not all the same: there is an inner core, which is solid, and an outer core that is like thick liquid.

INGE LEHMANN

LIVED: 1888–1993

NATIONALITY: Danish

FAMOUS FOR: Discovering that Earth's core is divided into an inner and an outer core

DID YOU KNOW? Lehmann retired from her work in Denmark in 1953 when she was 65, but then she moved to the United States and began a whole new research career. She worked for over 20 years in the USA, and lived on to the age of 105.

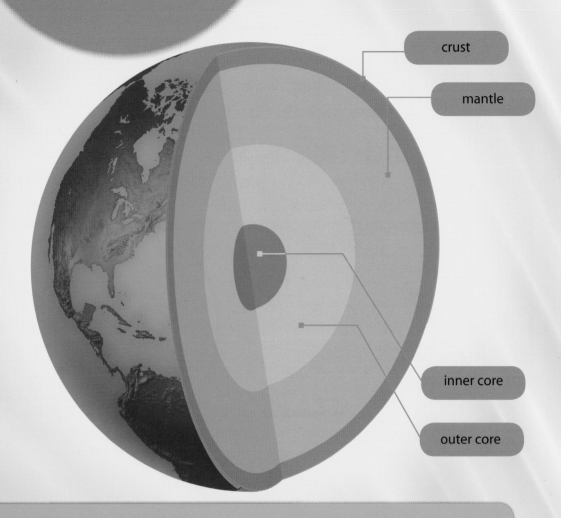

This cutaway diagram of Earth shows its structure. Lehmann made the discovery that Earth has an inner and an outer core.

crust

mantle

inner core

outer core

EARTH'S STRUCTURE

Earth's **crust** (surface layer) is many kilometres deep. However, compared to Earth's overall size, it is very thin. If Earth were the size of an apple, the crust would be about as thick as an apple's skin. Below the crust is the mantle, where the rocks are very hot. The mantle rocks can move very slowly, like thick sludge.

The mantle is nearly 3,000 kilometres (1,865 miles) thick. Below it is Earth's core, which is rich in the metals iron and nickel. The heat in the rocks comes from radioactivity in the core.

LANDS ON THE MOVE

While Inge Lehmann was still finishing her university studies, a German scientist called Alfred Wegener put forward a bold new idea that was years before its time.

NOT A REAL GEOLOGIST?

Alfred Wegener trained as a meteorologist – he studied the **atmosphere** and the weather. Wegener was especially interested in the Arctic atmosphere. He went on several scientific expeditions to the Greenland ice sheet.

Some time in 1910, Wegener became interested in the fact that the coasts of Africa and South America seem to fit together like pieces of a puzzle. Other people had noticed this before, but Wegener was fascinated. He began researching, and found other connections. Almost identical fossils were found in parts of South America and Africa. There were some rock formations that were very alike, too.

CONTINENTAL DRIFT

It was not only Africa and South America that had similarities. There were connections between other continents. In 1912 Wegener suggested a startling new theory to explain these findings. His idea was simple. The continents seemed to fit together because, at one time, they had been joined together! Millions of years ago, all the continents were part of a huge super-continent that Wegener called Pangaea. This super-continent then split up, and very slowly the pieces drifted to the positions they are in today.

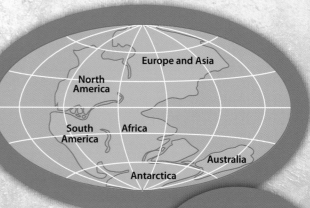

This is a reconstruction of how the continents all joined together to form Pangaea about 250 million years ago.

HOW MOUNTAINS FORM

Wegener suggested that continental drift could explain how mountains form. If two continents collided in a slow-motion crash, the land would buckle and fold, forming mountains. We know today that many mountains do form this way.

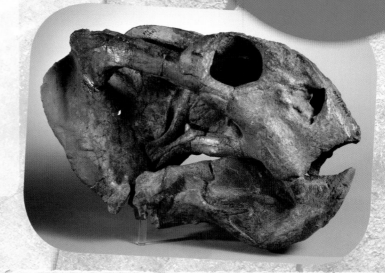

This is the fossil skull of a dicynodont, a kind of tusked dinosaur. Similar fossils are found in Australia, South America, and Africa.

ALFRED WEGENER

LIVED: 1880–1930

NATIONALITY: German

FAMOUS FOR: Suggesting that the continents can move

DID YOU KNOW? Wegener died on an expedition to Greenland that he was leading. He and two others tried to take supplies to a research station that did not have enough food for the winter. He reached the station and started back, but died in a storm on the return trip.

NO GOOD REASON

Wegener produced plenty of evidence for his continental drift theory. However, other scientists thought the idea was ridiculous. Part of the problem was that no one could explain how the continents moved.

Since Wegener's time, scientists have found the answer to how the continents move. (There is more about this in the next chapter.) They now know that a single continent of Pangaea did exist about 250 million years ago. But before Pangaea, there were at least two earlier super-continents. <u>The whole way through Earth's history, the land has joined into large masses and then broken up into smaller pieces.</u>

FUTURE DRIFT

Some scientists working today have used past land movements to predict how the continents will change in the future. Chris Hartnady in South Africa, Roy Livermore in the United Kingdom, and Christopher Scotese in the United States have developed different versions of what might happen. Hartnady predicts a super-continent called Amasia, which will not include Antarctica. Livermore thinks that Antarctica will be part of the next super-continent (called Novopangaea). Scotese's super-continent (called Pangaea Proxima) includes Antarctica and has a large inland sea.

All three models of the future are possible. Only time will tell if any are correct.

This is an illustration of how the world might look 250 million years from now.

FOSSIL MAGNETS

Earth is a giant magnet, but its magnetic field (the region where its magnetic force can be felt) is not fixed. The position of the north and south poles moves slightly all the time. Every so often, the north and south poles change places completely.

Some kinds of rock are magnetized as they form, and the magnetism becomes "locked in". The "fossil magnets" in the rocks always point to where the poles were when the rock formed. Fossil magnets in rocks from 250 million years ago point in many different directions. They do not all point to one north pole. However, if the continents are moved to the positions they had in Pangaea, the fossil magnets line up and point in the same direction.

Some of the rocks in the seafloor are fossil magnets. Scientists studying seafloor rocks have found that the magnetic field in the rocks is "striped" – pointing one way in one stripe, and the opposite way in the next stripe. The rocks record changes in the direction of Earth's magnetic field.

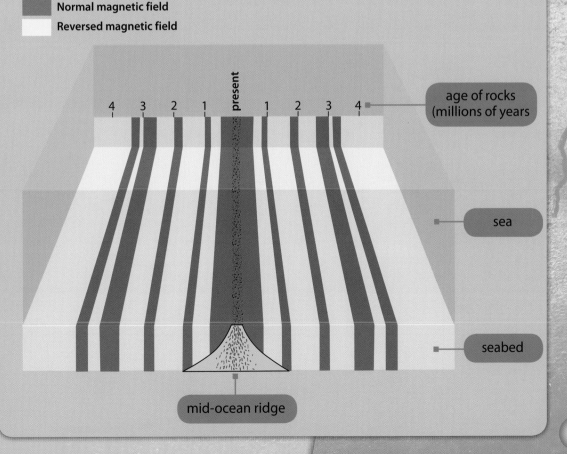

■ Normal magnetic field
□ Reversed magnetic field

present

4 3 2 1 1 2 3 4

age of rocks (millions of years

sea

seabed

mid-ocean ridge

MOUNTAINS
in the ocean

During World War II, a US Navy captain called Harry Hess began detailed surveys of the ocean floor. Just after the war, in 1947, a team funded by the US National Geographic Society also began surveying the ocean. The results of these surveys made the ocean floor suddenly very interesting.

Before this time, scientists thought that the ocean floor was very ancient. They expected to find the rocks covered by billions of years of sediment. In fact, the surveys found only a few million years' worth of sediment. Why was this? Was the ocean floor much younger than people had thought?

Scientists work on ocean survey ships like this one to find out more about Earth's processes.

MAPPING THE OCEANS

Two young scientists, Bruce Heezen and Marie Tharp, were given the job of making a map of the ocean floor, based on the information from survey ships. Tharp spent several years plotting the shape of small sections of the ocean floor and piecing them together. The complete map was published in 1957.

The most striking thing on the ocean floor map was a long chain of underwater mountains, running down the middle of the Atlantic Ocean, through the Southern (Antarctic) Ocean, and up into the Pacific Ocean. This chain of mountains connected all the way round the world, like the seam on a tennis ball.

Tharp was the first to suggest that it was not actually the mountains that connected together, but a deep valley running between the mountain ranges. Other research soon confirmed that Tharp was right. Many earthquakes happened along the line of this valley.

MARIE THARP

LIVED:	1920–2006
NATIONALITY:	American
FAMOUS FOR:	Mapping the ocean floor
DID YOU KNOW?	At the time that Tharp was working, women scientists were treated differently from men. Bruce Heezen made many trips on survey ships, but Tharp was not allowed. (She eventually got to make a trip in 1965.) When Tharp suggested that the divide down the centre of the mountain ranges was important, Heezen dismissed the idea. He said it was "girl talk".

FINDING AN EXPLANATION

Tharp and Heezen's map of the ocean floor showed very clearly a "seam" running right through all the oceans. But what did this mean? In 1962 Harry Hess suggested an explanation. The oceans were gradually getting wider! The long mountain chain was a crack in Earth's crust that was constantly opening up. As the crack opened, **molten** rock came up through it. This molten rock created the central valley and its surrounding mountains.

THE LONGEST MOUNTAIN CHAIN IN THE WORLD

The system of mid-ocean ridges together make up the longest mountain chain in the world. This underwater mountain chain is over 80,000 kilometres (50,000 miles) long.

This is the map of the ocean beds made by Marie Tharp and her colleagues. The dark lines indicate the ocean ridges.

AN ACCEPTED THEORY

If Hess was right, seafloor spreading would help explain how continental drift happened. <u>The continents moved apart because an ocean opened up between them</u>. Most geologists still did not accept the idea of continental drift. However, within two years, evidence such as the magnetic stripes in seafloor rocks (see the diagram on page 27) came along to back up Tharp and Heezen's map. The idea of seafloor spreading was accepted.

SUBMARINE SURVEYS

In the 1970s, scientists predicted that hot springs (geothermal vents) would be found along the mid-ocean ridges, where molten rock was erupting from below the surface. A hot spring was detected in 1976, and in 1977 a submersible (small submarine) called *Alvin* went down to investigate. When *Alvin* reached the geothermal vent, scientists were amazed to find **bacteria**, worms, crabs, and many other living things that had adapted to live in this extreme environment.

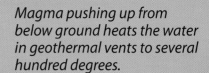

Scientists can do different kinds of underwater research using the submersible *Alvin*.

PLATE TECTONICS

Once scientists accepted that seafloor spreading was happening, Wegener's theory of continental drift was more widely accepted. But there were still many problems with the idea. One important question was: why are the oceans expanding? Another puzzle was: if the oceans are constantly producing new crust and getting wider, somewhere else Earth's crust must be disappearing. Otherwise, Earth would be gradually expanding.

In the 1960s, a Canadian scientist called Tuzo Wilson brought together seafloor spreading, continental drift, and other evidence into one theory – **plate tectonics**.

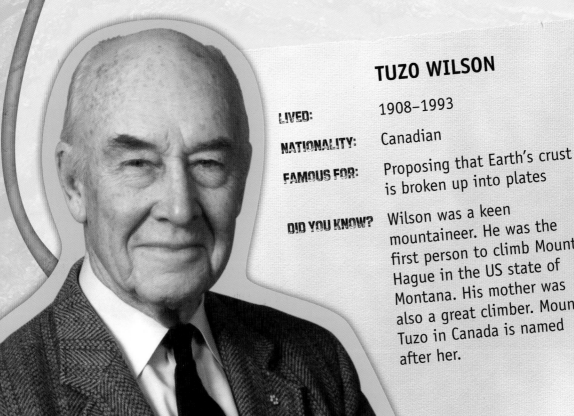

TUZO WILSON

LIVED:	1908–1993
NATIONALITY:	Canadian
FAMOUS FOR:	Proposing that Earth's crust is broken up into plates
DID YOU KNOW?	Wilson was a keen mountaineer. He was the first person to climb Mount Hague in the US state of Montana. His mother was also a great climber. Mount Tuzo in Canada is named after her.

A CRACKED EGG

Wilson suggested that Earth's crust was not one piece: it was broken up into several pieces, like a cracked eggshell. These pieces are called plates.

The plates of Earth's crust are not still. They move very, very slowly, carried by movements of the mantle below. In some places, two plates are moving apart from each other. This is what is happening in the middle of the oceans. At the edges of the oceans, the ocean plates are crashing slowly into the continents. Where this happens, the ocean floor gets pushed underneath the continental rocks. As the ocean floor sinks deeper and deeper, it gradually melts. Then new ocean crust is created in the middle of the oceans, while old ocean crust disappears around the ocean fringes.

In some places, the plates are not crashing into each other or moving apart. They are moving side by side, in opposite directions. One region like this is the San Andreas Fault in California, USA.

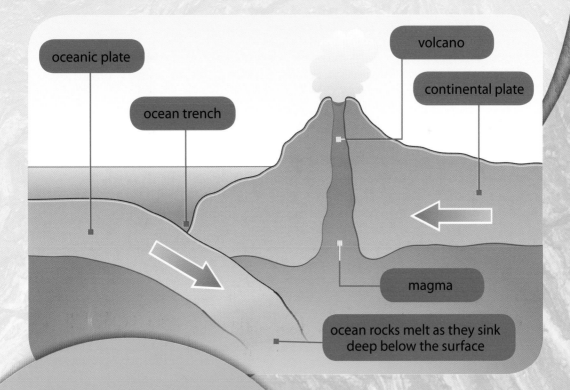

oceanic plate

volcano

continental plate

ocean trench

magma

ocean rocks melt as they sink deep below the surface

Where an ocean plate crashes into a continent, the heavy rocks of the ocean bed sink under the continental rocks. Mountains and volcanoes form just behind the "crash zone".

VOLCANOES AND EARTHQUAKES

Earthquakes and volcanoes do not occur everywhere on Earth. They are concentrated in narrow bands. For example, there are earthquakes all down the west coast of South America, and along a line from northern Russia southwards to Japan, then across to New Zealand. Volcanoes occur in these areas, too.

All these earthquake and volcano zones are along plate boundaries. Wherever one plate meets another, Earth's crust is under stress. New rocks are being made, or old rocks are being crushed or melted. These stresses produce volcanoes and earthquakes.

HOT SPOTS

In a few places, there are volcanoes in places where there is no plate boundary. These are known as hot spots. The volcanoes of Hawaii, for example, are caused by a hot spot.

In the early 1960s, Tuzo Wilson studied the volcanoes of Hawaii. He found that the Hawaiian Islands were part of a long chain of islands stretching across the Pacific Ocean to Russia. Each of these islands was formed by volcanoes pushing up from under the sea. After a few thousand years the volcanoes became dormant (inactive). Wilson suggested that the islands had all been formed by the same hot spot. The hot spot had stayed in the same place beneath Earth's crust, but the crust above it had moved. This meant that instead of just one island, a whole chain was formed as the ocean plate moved over the hot spot.

The Hawaiian Islands form a long line, showing the movement of the ocean crust above the hot spot deep below.

MOUNTAIN-BUILDING

When two plates collide, mountain ranges form.
When two land plates collide, this produces the
biggest mountains. The biggest "crash" happening
today is where the Indian plate is colliding with
Asia. This has produced the Himalayan Mountains.

Himalayan Mountains

Predicting the weather

Alfred Wegener is best known today for his continental drift theory. But his "real job" was studying the weather. In Wegener's time, researchers did many studies of the atmosphere and the water cycle. However, weather forecasting remained very inaccurate.

Then, in the 1960s, a US meteorologist made a strange discovery. He showed that forecasting the weather could never be really accurate. His discoveries led to modern forecasting methods, which use computer "models" of the world's weather systems.

EDWARD LORENZ

LIVED: 1917–2008

NATIONALITY: American

FAMOUS FOR: Discovering that tiny changes in the atmosphere can produce huge changes in the weather. This became known as **chaos theory** (see page 38).

DID YOU KNOW? Lorenz once gave a talk on chaos theory called "Does the Flap of a Butterfly's Wings in Brazil Set off a Tornado in Texas?" The flap of a butterfly's wings causes a really tiny change in the air. But even such a small change could set off large-scale changes in the weather. After this talk, chaos theory became known as "the butterfly effect".

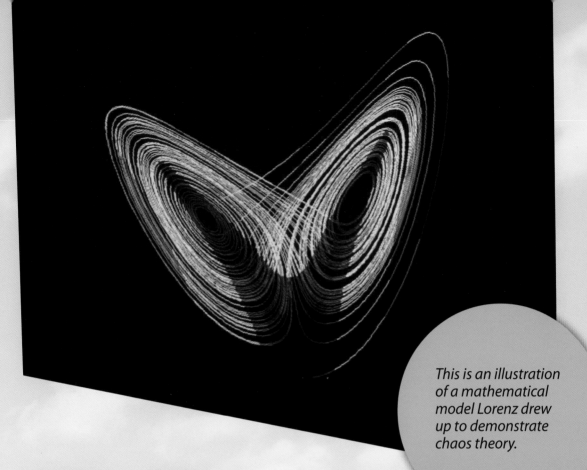

This is an illustration of a mathematical model Lorenz drew up to demonstrate chaos theory.

CHECKING A MODEL

In 1961 Edward Lorenz was making computer models of the atmosphere. (A computer model is a program that behaves as far as possible like the actual atmosphere.) Lorenz was testing out a program by feeding in some **data** (real information about the weather). He ran the program once, and then he did a repeat run. The second time, the results were completely different.

Lorenz checked back to see what had gone wrong. The only difference he found was that on the second run he had typed in the data from a printout. The numbers in the printout were slightly less accurate than the originals. But the differences were less than one part in 1,000. Lorenz was puzzled: how could such tiny differences in the data cause such big differences in the end result?

Turn the page to find out what Lorenz discovered ...

CHAOS THEORY

Lorenz realized that the reason for the big difference was not a mistake: it was caused by his computer model. Very slight differences in the initial data could produce very large differences in the final results.

Lorenz went on to show that the effect he had seen in his computer program applied to real weather situations. So, <u>atmospheric conditions that are almost the same can lead to a storm on one occasion and a heatwave on another.</u> This is the discovery Lorenz called chaos theory.

What Lorenz had shown was that it was impossible to accurately predict the weather. Really tiny changes in the atmosphere, or in other conditions, could completely change what the weather was like.

Japanese meteorologist Syukuro Manabe (born 1931) was one of the first to use computers to build models of the global climate.

COMPUTER POWER

Scientists are constantly looking for more computing power to improve weather forecasting. Supercomputers used at the National Oceanic and Atmospheric Administration in the United States can make 70 trillion calculations per second.

Better weather models help to improve longer-term forecasts of the climate. These are very important for studying climate change.

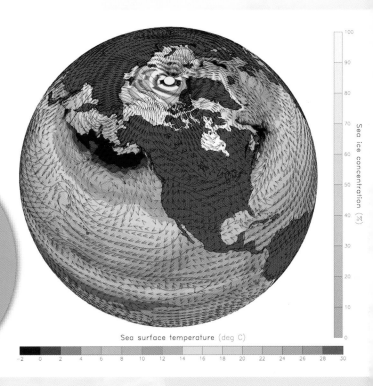

This computer model shows the temperature of the sea and areas of sea ice. The grey areas are land.

Sea ice concentration (%)

Sea surface temperature (deg C)

-2   0   2   4   6   8   10   12   14   16   18   20   22   24   26   28   30

MODERN WEATHER FORECASTING

Chaos theory limits how accurately we can forecast the weather. However, it is possible to work round the problem to produce fairly good forecasts over two or three days.

To do this, modern forecasters use huge amounts of computing power. They collect information about current conditions from weather stations on the ground, balloons in the air, and satellites in space. This is all fed into complex computer models of the weather. Forecasters feed the data into several different computer models. They run each model several times, each time with slightly different starting conditions. This gives a spread of different results. Forecasters then produce a "best fit" forecast from all the results.

What next?

The work of pioneering scientists has completely changed our understanding of Earth and how it works. We have learned about the history of Earth itself, how life developed and changed, and changes in the weather and climate.

We have learned a lot, but today's geologists and earth scientists still have plenty to discover. One growing area of research is other planets and moons. There have been many exciting discoveries in this area. A space probe (unmanned spacecraft) called *Galileo* discovered thousands of volcanoes on Io, one of Jupiter's moons.

Scientists thought that Io should be dead and cold, like Earth's moon. However, the gravitational pull of Jupiter and other moons twist and distort Io, heating up the rocks and producing thousands of volcanoes.

Dr Claudia Alexander is a geophysicist who works for the US National Aeronautics and Space Administration. She was manager of part of the Galileo space mission, which sent back amazing pictures of volcanoes on Io.

LIFE AT THE EXTREMES

Geoscience professor Tullis Onstott is interested in whether there is life in space. He tries to find out by looking in the most unlikely place: deep under ground on Earth.

In 2006 Onstott and a team of scientists from Princeton University in the United States found bacteria living in rocks over 3 kilometres (2 miles) under ground. The bacteria get their energy from radioactivity in the rocks around them, rather than from food or sunlight. Onstott believes that finding life in such extreme conditions on Earth makes it far more likely that we will find living things in the extreme environments of other planets.

HUMAN IMPACT

One of the biggest questions today is how Earth's processes are being affected by humans. How much do the smoke and gases from factories and cars affect the atmosphere and the oceans? What changes have they made to the climate? What effects will humans have in the future?

One thing we know from Lorenz's chaos theory: the future is impossible to predict. But with enough understanding of Earth's processes, we can reduce our impact on Earth and learn how to change things for the better.

TIMELINE

Follow the coloured arrows to see how some of the ideas and discoveries of earth scientists influenced other scientists.

James Hutton
(1726–1797)

proposed that some rocks were formed by heat (melting); the principle that processes observed acting on rocks today can explain what happened to rocks in the past; that the age of Earth is millions of years, not thousands.

Charles Lyell
(1797–1875)

promoted geology, especially Hutton's ideas.

Louis Agassiz
(1807–1893)

found evidence that glaciers were more widespread in the past.

William Smith
(1769–1829)

showed how fossils could be used to date rocks. Produced first geological map of Britain.

Alfred Wegener
(1880–1930)

proposed theory of continental drift.

Tuzo Wilson
(1908–1993)
developed theory of
plate tectonics.

Edward Lorenz
(1917–2008)
developed chaos
theory – the idea
that tiny changes in
the atmosphere can
produce huge changes
in the weather.

Xu Xing
(born 1969)
has discovered many
dinosaur fossils that
show the connection
between dinosaurs and
birds.

Arthur Holmes
(1890–1965)
developed process of
radioactive dating of
rocks.

**Christopher
Scotese**
(born 1953)
modelled future
changes in positions of
continents.

Inge Lehmann
(1888–1993)
used studies of
seismic waves to
show that Earth had
an inner core.

Marie Tharp
(1920–2006)
made first ocean floor
map of world, showing
presence of mid-ocean
ridges.

Joseph Kirschvink
(born 1953)
proposed "Snowball
Earth" idea.

Quick quiz

1 **What do meteorologists study?**

(a) distance in meters
(b) meteors
(c) the weather

2 **Who used a meteorite to estimate the age of the Earth?**

(a) David Cameron
(b) Clair Cameron Patterson
(c) Charles Patterson

3 **What theory did James Hutton draw up?**

(a) theory of Noah's Flood
(b) theory of the Earth
(c) theory of the rock cycle

4 **How many fossils has Xu Xing discovered?**

(a) one or two
(b) a dozen
(c) more than 30

5 **What is *Alvin* used for?**

(a) mountain rescue
(b) weather forecasting
(c) underwater research

6 **What theory shows that it is impossible to predict the weather accurately?**

(a) theory of the Earth
(b) chaos theory
(c) theory of evolution

Answers: 1 (c), **2** (b), **3** (b), **4** (c), **5** (c), **6** (b)

Glossary

atmosphere layer of air that blankets Earth

bacteria microscopic living things made up of a single, very simple cell

chaos theory the idea that, in systems such as the weather, a very small difference between starting conditions can produce very different outcomes

climate average weather in a region, over many years

climatologist scientist who studies the climate

core central part of Earth

crust rocky outer surface layer of Earth

data information, usually numbers of some kind

forecast predict or suggest what might happen

fossil remains of a long-dead living thing found in rocks

geologist scientist who studies rocks

glacier "river" of ice, that flows very slowly downwards under the pull of gravity

mantle layer of hot rock beneath Earth's crust

meteorologist scientist who studies the weather

molten melted, liquid

palaeontologist scientist who studies fossils to learn about the history of life on Earth

plate tectonics the theory that Earth's crust is broken into large pieces called plates, which move very slowly

radioactive sends out energy in strong waves

sedimentary rock type of rock formed from sediments that have been compressed (squashed together)

sediments small particles of rock and other material. Sediments can range from gravel (fairly large pieces) through sand and silt, to mud (very fine, tiny particles).

seismic wave vibration that is produced by earthquakes and travels through the rocks below ground or along Earth's surface

uplift process of lifting up whole areas of Earth's surface. Uplift often happens when two pieces of crust collide.

Find out more

Books

Alfred Wegener (Makers of Modern Science), Lisa Yount (Chelsea House Publishers, 2009)

The Earth: An Intimate History, Richard Fortey (HarperPerennial, 2005)

Earth's Cycles and Systems (Sci-Hi), Andrew Solway (Raintree, 2010)

Earth Science (Pioneers in Science series), Katherine Cullen, Scott McCutcheon and Bobbi McCutcheon (Facts On File, 2006)

Earth's Shifting Surface (Sci-Hi), Robert Snedden (Raintree, 2010)

Websites

This dynamic earth:
pubs.usgs.gov/gip/dynamic/dynamic.html
An online version of a booklet about plate tectonics from the US Geological Survey (USGS). If you want to learn more about plate tectonics, this is a great place to start.

The water cycle:
ga.water.usgs.gov/edu/watercycle.html
Another good USGS website, this time about the water cycle.

The Lorenz butterfly:
www.exploratorium.edu/complexity/java/lorenz.html
Try chaos theory for yourself. Set off two "particles" on a journey, and see how they are soon travelling on very different paths, no matter how close together they started.

Paleomap Project:
www.scotese.com
Want to see how Pangaea looked, or how Earth might look 50 million years from now? This is the place to go!

Topics to research

Rocks
Find examples of the different kinds of rocks: sedimentary, igneous, and metamorphic.

Climate change
Check out debates about climate change. What will happen after our current ice age? Is Earth's climate getting warmer? Do you think this is because of the way humans live or because it is part of Earth's processes?

Fossils
Go on an organized fossil-hunting tour. Be sure to follow the Geographical Fieldwork Code available at:
www.geolsoc.org.uk/gsl/site/GSL/lang/en/page2542.html

"Dinosaur City"
Find out about the thousands of fossils found near the city of Zhucheng in China, a place that has become known as "Dinosaur City".

Jurassic Park?
Find a geological timeline and work out when the Jurassic Period was. What happened to the supercontinent Pangaea during this time? What kind of dinosaurs lived then?

Index

Agassiz, Louis 12–13, 14, 16, 42
age of the Earth 6, 10
Alexander, Claudia 41
Amasia 26
Anchiornis 19
Antarctic 14, 15, 26
Arctic 24
atmosphere 24, 36, 38

bacteria 31, 41
biologists 13
birds 18, 19

chaos theory 36, 37, 38, 39, 41
climate change 12, 14, 39
climatologists 5
computer models 36, 37, 38, 39
continental drift 24, 25, 26, 30, 32
core, Earth's 20, 22, 23
crust, Earth's 21, 23, 30, 32, 33, 34

dicynodont 25
dinosaurs 18, 19, 25

earthquakes 20, 22, 29, 34
erosion 10
erratics 13
evolutionary theory 13

fossil feathers 19
fossil magnets 27
fossil signatures 16
fossils 4, 5, 8, 14, 16–18, 24, 25

geologists 4, 6, 8–11, 30
geothermal vents 31
glacials 15
glaciers 12, 13
Grand Canyon 7
Greenland 13, 24, 25
Gutenberg, Beno 20

Hartnady, Chris 26
Hawaiian Islands 34
Heezen, Bruce 29, 30
Hess, Harry 30
Himalayan Mountains 35
Holmes, Arthur 6, 43
hot spots 34
hurricanes 5
Hutton, James 8, 9, 10, 20, 42

ice ages 13, 14, 15
ice caps 13
ice cores 14, 15
ice sheets 15, 24
igneous rocks 8
interglacials 15
iron 23

Kirschvink, Joseph 15, 43
Kola Superdeep Borehole 21

Lehman, Inge 22, 23, 43
Livermore, Roy 26
Lorenz, Edward 36, 37, 38, 43
Lyell, Charles 10, 11, 42

magnetic fields 27
Manabe, Syukuro 38
mantle, Earth's 20, 23, 33
meteorologists 5, 24, 36, 38
Microraptor 19
mid-ocean ridges 30, 31
Mohorovičić, Andrija 20
molten rock 30, 31
moons 40, 41
mountains 25, 29, 30, 33, 35

naturalists 12
nickel 23
Noah's Flood 6, 8, 10
north and south poles 27
Novopangaea 26

Onstott, Tullis 41

palaeontologists 5, 18, 19
Pangaea 24, 26, 27

Pangaea Proxima 26
Patterson, Clair Cameron 6
plate tectonics 32–33, 34, 35

radioactivity 6, 23, 41
rock cycle 10
rocks 4, 6, 7, 8, 10, 13, 14, 16, 17, 23, 27, 30, 31, 34, 41

San Andreas Fault 33
satellites 5, 39
Scotese, Christopher 26, 43
seabed 21, 27, 28–31, 33
seafloor spreading 30, 32
sediment 8, 28
sedimentary rocks 8, 16
seismic waves (shock waves) 20, 21, 22
seismographs 22
seismologists 22
Smith, William 16–17, 18, 42
"Snowball Earth" theory 15
super-continents 24, 26

Tharp, Marie 29, 30, 43
Theory of the Earth 9, 10

uplift 8, 10

valleys 13, 29, 30
volcanoes 20, 33, 34, 40

weather 5, 24, 36–39
weather forecasting 36, 38, 39
weathering 10
Wegener, Alfred 24, 25, 26, 36, 42
Werner, Abraham 8
Wilson, Tuzo 32–33, 34, 43
women scientists 22, 29, 41, 43

Xu Xing 18, 19, 43